The Spiritual

A BOOK

ARIEL BOOKS

ANDREWS AND MCMEEL
KANSAS CITY

ISBN: 0-8362-0724-6

Library of Congress Catalog Card Number: 95-76439

The Spiritual Life

❧

Introduction

_ক্স_

$\mathcal{A}$ spiritual awakening ... it can happen when we least expect it. Walking through a park, laughing with colleagues, or drinking coffee at an outdoor cafe, we suddenly experience a feeling of happiness, of love for others, of connection between ourselves and the world at large. These are usually private revelations, whose occurrence remains unknown to those around us. We feel a deep gratitude for life and all of its many blessings, great and small. As Walt Whitman says, ". . . a leaf of grass is no less than the journeywork of the stars . . ."

Faith, hope, and love fuse together to form a new reality. Washing the dishes, drafting a proposal at work, walking the dog in the evening—it's as if we are doing these things for the first time. The glories of the world are revealed in all their complexity and all their simplicity.

Perhaps most important, we find our soul. This has less to do with religion, catechisms, and Sunday worship and more to do with discovering our spiritual nature. With this knowledge emerges a new respect for ourselves and for others. We begin to understand the sacredness of all people and all things. The beautiful tree on the edge of a hill is as alive as the red fox running through the forest. As you read the poets, gurus, and public leaders quoted in this book, don't be surprised if your own spirituality begins to awaken.

For nowhere can a mind find a retreat more full of peace or more free from care than his own soul.

※

Marcus Aurelius

I do not know what I may appear to the world, but to myself I seem to have been only like a boy playing on the seashore and diverting myself in now and then finding a smoother pebble or a prettier shell than ordinary, whilst the great ocean of truth lay all undiscovered before me.

∞

Sir Isaac Newton

It isn't until you come to a spiritual
understanding of who you are—
not necessarily a religious feeling,
but deep down, the spirit within—
that you can begin to take control.

❧

Oprah Winfrey

Soul is the Man.

⚬⚬

Thomas Campion

Let your soul stand cool and composed before a million universes.

— ✦ —

Walt Whitman

No one draws closer to a knowledge of the truth than he who has advanced far in the knowledge of divine things, and yet knows that something always remains for him to seek.

St. Leo

A contented mind is the greatest
blessing a man can enjoy in this world;
and if, in the present life, his happiness arises
from the subduing of his desires, it will rise
to the next from the gratification of them.

ᔕᔕ

Joseph Addison

*The turning point
in the process of growing up
is when you discover the core
of strength within you that
survives all hurt.*

❦

Max Lerner

$\mathcal{R}$adar may make possible the avoidance of unseen dangers for plane, ship, and car. Radar of the spirit may enable man, in time, to avoid war, forms of disease, and sins of selfishness, arrogance, and pride. Radar of the spirit may tap resources of spiritual power long dreamed of, but never made widely available to man. Such power may send man over the mountains of racial antagonism, social and economic barriers, and denominational differences.

Arthur L. Miller

Spiritual and religious traditions, when shaped by the feminine principle, affirm the cyclical phases of our lives and the wisdom each phase brings, the sacredness of our bodies and the body of the Earth.

Patrice Wynne

The Kingdom of God is within you.

— ❧ —

Luke 17:21

Turn not to the outside world! Into thine own self go back! In the inner man alone resides truth.

— ∞ —

St. Augustine

God is an utterable sigh,
planted in the depths
of the soul.

— ❧ —

Jean Paul Richter

There is in every true woman's heart
a spark of heavenly fire, which lies dormant
in the broad daylight of prosperity, but
which kindles up, and beams and blazes in
the dark hour of adversity.

&

Washington Irving

In this world it is not what
we take up,
but what we give up, that
makes us rich.

———— ✹ ————

Henry Ward Beecher

Try to keep your soul young and quivering right up to old age, and to imagine right up to the brink of death that life is only beginning. I think that is the only way to keep adding to one's talent, to one's affections, and one's inner happiness.

൧൦

George Sand

*Spirituality is as much
an ability to accept love as
it is a capacity for loving.*

———— ∞ ————

Francine du Plessix Gray

God, I can push the grass apart And lay my finger on Thy heart!

Edna St. Vincent Millay

The tragedy of life is not death but in what dies inside a man while he lives—the death of genuine feeling, the death of inspired response, the death of the awareness that makes it possible to feel that pain or the glory of other men in oneself.

ഇൻ

Norman Cousins

All prayers are answered. We need to
distinguish between a prayer unanswered
and one not answered how or when we
would like it to be.

જજ

Lloyd Ogilvie

Religion is something infinitely simple, ingenuous.... In the infinite extent of the universe, it is a direction of the heart.

—⚭—

Rainer Maria Rilke

Life is a pure flame, and

we live by an

invisible sun within us.

———— ∞ ————

Sir Thomas Browne

Spirituality lies in regarding existence merely as a vehicle for contemplation, and contemplation merely as a vehicle for joy.

George Santayana

Give to the world the best you have and the best will come back to you.

———— ✦ ————

Anonymous

Make a prayer acknowledging yourself as a vehicle of light, giving thanks for the good that has come that day and an affirmation of intent to live in harmony with all your relations.

ॐ

Dhyani Ywahoo

It is not the eye that sees the beauty of the heaven, nor the ear that hears the sweetness of music or the glad tidings of a prosperous occurrence, but the soul, that perceives all the relishes of sensual and intellectual perfections; and the more noble and excellent the soul is, the greater and more savory are its perceptions.

Jeremy Taylor

The soul is the mirror of

an indestructible

universe.

— ∞ —

Gottfried Wilhelm

von Leibnitz

That is happiness: to be dissolved into something complete and great.

— ✠ —

Willa Cather

The good neighbor looks beyond
the external accidents and discerns
those inner qualities that make all men
human and, therefore, brothers.

ℬ

Martin Luther King, Jr.

He that sees the beauty of holiness, or true moral good, sees the greatest and most important thing in the world. . . . There is no other true excellence or beauty.

୨୪

Jonathan Edwards

A contented spirit is the sweetness of existence.

— ❧ —

Anonymous

Let us keep open the connections whereby the human spirit may freely move between the arts and the sciences and thus make more of each. May we thus become better violinists, scientists, artists, writers, and above all, better human beings, by enlarging and enriching our personal needs to include each other's.

Yehudi Menuhin

In a world of prayer, we are all equal in
the sense that each of us is a unique person,
with a unique perspective on the world,
a member of a class of one.

ഇരു

W. H. Auden

It is not the number of books you read,
nor the variety of sermons you hear,
nor the amount of religious conversation
in which you mix, but it is the frequency
and earnestness with which you meditate
on these things till the truth in them
becomes your own and part of your being,
that ensures your growth.

ℒℴ

Frederick William Robertson

Every human being has been brought into the world according to the will of God. And God created us in such a way that every human being can either save his own soul or destroy it. Man's task in life is to save his soul. In order to save our souls, we must live according to the ways of God, and in order to live according to the ways of God, we must renounce the sensual pleasures of life; we must labor, suffer and be kind and humble.

Leo Tolstoy

Faith is the subtle chain
Which binds us to the infinite; the voice
Of a deep life within, that will remain
Until we crowd it thence.

☙

Elizabeth Oakes Smith

All is miracle. The stupendous order of nature, the revolution of a hundred millions of worlds around a million of suns, the activity of light, the life of animals, all are grand and perpetual miracles.

Voltaire

Prayer is the contemplation of the facts of life from the highest point of view.

❧

Ralph Waldo Emerson

Of all things which a man has, next to the gods, his soul is the most divine and most truly his own.

വ

Plato

Let us open up our natures, throw wide
the doors of our hearts and let in the
sunshine of good will and kindness.

ঞ

O. S. Marden

The way to God is by ourselves.

❧

Phineas Fletcher

Depend upon it, it is not the want of greater miracles but of the soul to perceive such as are allowed us still, that makes us push all the sanctities into the far spaces we cannot reach. The devout feel that wherever God's hand is, *there* is miracle.

ᘉᘉ

James Martineau

The spiritual life ... means the ever more perfect and willing association of the invisible Divine Spirit for all purposes; for the glory of God, for the growth and culture of the praying soul.

ಬಿ

Evelyn Underhill

There is one spectacle grander than the sea, that is the sky; there is one spectacle grander than the sky, that is the interior of the soul.

—— ✦ ——

Victor Hugo

And why pierceth it heaven, this little short prayer of one syllable [God]? for it is prayed with a full spirit, in the height and in the depth, in the length and in the breadth of his spirit that prayeth it.

∞

The Cloud of Unknowing

Faith is the pencil of the soul that pictures heavenly things.

— ✼ —

Thomas Burbridge

Your prayer must be that you may have a
sound mind in a sound body. Pray for a
bold spirit, free from all dread of death; that
reckons the closing scene of life among
Nature's kindly boons.

❧

Juvenal

That deep emotional conviction of the presence of a superior reasoning power, which is revealed in the incomprehensible universe, forms my idea of God.

℘℘

Albert Einstein

The soul of man is larger than the sky,
Deeper than ocean, or abysmal dark
Of the unfathomed centre.

෨

Hartley Coleridge

To accept what you are is to be content, and contentment is the greatest wealth. To work with patience is to gather power. To surrender to the Eternal flow is to be completely present.

Vimala McClure

Invest in the human soul.
Who knows, it might be a
diamond in the rough.

— ✠ —

Mary McLeod Bethune

Love is a desire of the whole being
to be united to some thing, or some being,
felt necessary to its completeness, by the
most perfect means that nature permits,
and reason dictates.

∞

Samuel Taylor Coleridge

It seems to me as if not only the form but the soul of man was made to walk erect and look upon the stars.

— ☙ —

John Bulwer

One must have lived
greatly whose record would
bear the full light of day
from beginning to its close.

——— ∾ ———

A. Bronson Alcott

Prayer is the peace of our spirit,
the stillness of our thoughts, the evenness
of our recollection, the sea of our
meditation, the rest of our cares,
and the calm of our tempest.

ഗ

Jeremy Taylor

Learn to get in touch with silence within yourself and know that everything in this life has a purpose. There are no mistakes, no coincidences, all events are blessings given to us to learn from.

ဆ

Elisabeth Kübler-Ross

Confront the dark parts of yourself, and work to banish them with illumination and forgiveness. Your willingness to wrestle with your demons will cause your angels to sing. Use the pain as fuel, as a reminder of your strength.

ა

August Wilson

Life is one long joy, because the will of God is always being done in it, and the glory of God always being got from it.

∞

F. W. Faber

Prayer is the most powerful form of
energy one can generate. The influence of
prayer on the human mind and body is as
demonstrable as that of the secreting glands.
Prayer is a force as real as terrestrial gravity.
It supplies us with a flow of sustaining
power in our daily lives.

∞

Alexis Carrel

To glorify God is to be engaged in a concrete spirituality that refuses to draw marked distinctions between sacred and secular, contemplation and deed, theology and ethics.

☙

Douglas John Hall

Wise men appreciate all men, for they see the good in each and know how hard it is to make anything good.

⚜

Baltasar Gracián

God's miracles are to be found in
nature itself; the wind and waves,
the wood that becomes a tree—all of these
are explained biologically, but behind them
is the hand of God. And I believe that is
true of creation itself.

ന

Ronald Reagan

A positive thing; in Joy one does not only feel secure, but something goes out from one's self to the universe, a warm, possessive effluence of love.

ↂ

John Buchan

No man is an island, entire of itself; every man is a piece of the continent, a part of the main. If a clod be washed away by the sea, Europe is the less, as well as if a promontory were, as well as if a manor of thy friend's or of thine own were. Any man's death diminishes me because I am involved in mankind ...

John Donne

Oh, write of me, not

"Died in bitter pains,"

But "Emigrated to

another star!"

— ❧ —

Helen Hunt Jackson

Prayer is exhaling the

spirit of man and

inhaling the spirit of God.

———— ∞ ————

Edwin Keith

Someone has said that all living is just learning the meaning of words. That does not mean the long ten-syllable words we have to look up in the dictionary. The really great words to master are short ones— work, love, hope, joy, pain, home, child, life, death.

ɞƆ

Halford E. Luccock

Make yourself familiar with the angels, and behold them frequently in spirit; for, without being seen, they are present with you.

❧

St. Francis de Sales

No man ever forgot the visitation of that power to his heart and brain, which created all things anew; which was the dawn in him of music, poetry, and art; which made the face of nature radiant with purple light, the morning and the night varied enchantments; when a single tone of one voice could make the heart bound.

Ralph Waldo Emerson

Possess your soul with patience.

❧

John Dryden

Spiritual love is a position of standing
with one hand extended into the universe
and one hand extended into the world,
letting ourselves be a conduit for
passing energy.

∞

Christina Baldwin

Man needs, for his happiness, not only the enjoyment of this or that, but hope and enterprise and change.

— ✍ —

Bertrand Russell

I swear I think now that everything without exception has an eternal soul! The trees have, rooted in the ground! the weeds of the sea have! the animals!

ॐ

Walt Whitman

There is only one such Self, and that one self is you. Standing behind this little nature is what we call the Soul. . . .

He is the Soul of your soul. . . .

You are one with Him.

ಹ

Swami Vivekananda

Compassion for myself is the most powerful healer of them all.

— ❧ —

Theodore Isaac Rubin

Seize upon truth, wherever it is found, amongst your friends, amongst your foes, on Christian or on heathen ground; the flower's divine where'er it grows.

ഇൻ

Isaac Watts

Whether or not the philosophers care to admit that we have a soul, it seems obvious that we are equipped with something or other which generates dreams and ideals, and which sets up values.

John Erskine

In the faces of men and women I see God and in my own face in the glass, I find letters from God dropt in the street, and every one is signed by God's name, and I leave them where they are, for I know that wheresoever I go others will punctually come for ever and ever.

Walt Whitman

My soul is myself; the well-spring or
point of consciousness, or center of inner
activity . . . the most real thing in the
universe to me; the start for all other
knowing, the test by which I judge
all other data.

ာ

Upton Sinclair

Nature: The Unseen Intelligence which loved us into being, and is disposing of us by the same token.

——— ℛ ———

Elbert Hubbard

I hold you here, root and all, in my hand,
Little flower—but *if* I could understand
What you are, root and all, and all in all,
I should know what God and man is.

ॐ

Alfred, Lord Tennyson

No man truly has joy
unless he lives in love.

— ❧ —

St. Thomas Aquinas

I could not say I believe. I know! I have had the experience of being gripped by something that is stronger than myself, something that people call God.

☙

Carl Jung

I would rather live in a world where my life is surrounded by mystery than live in a world so small that my mind could comprehend it.

෧෨

Harry Emerson Fosdick

There is, above all, the laughter that comes from the eternal joy of creation, the joy of making the world new, the joy of expressing the inner riches of the soul—laughter from triumphs over pain and hardship in the passion for an enduring ideal, the joy of bringing the light of happiness, of truth and beauty into a dark world. This is divine laughter par excellence.

John Elof Boodin

Be careless in your dress

if you must, but keep

a tidy soul.

— ❧ —

Mark Twain

All the kindness which a man puts
out into the world works on the heart
and thoughts of mankind.

ೞ

Albert Schweitzer

Love is the magician, the enchanter, that changes worthless things to joy, and makes right royal kings and queens of common clay. It is the perfume of that wondrous flower, the heart, and without that sacred passion, that divine swoon, we are less than beasts; but with it, earth is heaven, and we are gods.

Robert G. Ingersoll

To live happily is an inward power of the soul.

— ❧ —

Marcus Aurelius

When people universally realize that all are united by the common bond of mortality and by the basic needs ... the need to worship and to love, to be housed and fed, to work and play—perhaps we will have learned to understand—which is to love spiritually, and there will be peace and brotherhood on earth. Without brotherhood, peace is not possible

Faith Baldwin

Joy is the realization of the truth of one-ness, the oneness of our soul with the world and of the world-soul with the supreme love.

കൗ

Rabindranath Tagore

I loafe and invite

my soul,

I lean and loafe at my ease

observing a spear of

summer grass.

— ⚭ —

Walt Whitman

Hope is some extraordinary spiritual
grace that God gives us to control
our fears, not to oust them.

∞

Vincent McNabb

Follow your bliss.

— ❧ —

Joseph Campbell

Natural objects themselves, even when
they make no claim to beauty, excite the
feelings, and occupy the imagination.
Nature pleases, attracts, delights, merely
because it is nature. We recognize in it an
Infinite Power.

☙

Karl Wilhelm von Humboldt

Deep within us all there is an amazing inner sanctuary of the soul, a holy place, a Divine Center, a speaking Voice. . . . Life from the Center is a life of unhurried peace and power. It is simple. It is serene. It is amazing. It is radiant.

∽

T. R. Kelly

Every man recognizes within himself a free and rational spirit, independent of his body. This spirit is what we call God.

— Leo Tolstoy

Liberty of thought is the life of the soul.

— ✿ —

Voltaire

Hope ... is one of the ways in which what is merely future and potential is made vividly present and actual to us. Hope is the positive, as anxiety is the negative, mode of awaiting the future.

∞

Emil Brunner

Love all God's creation, the whole and every grain of sand in it. Love every leaf, every ray of God's light. Love the animals, love the plants, love everything. If you love everything, you will perceive the divine mystery in things. Once you perceive it, you will begin to comprehend it better every day. And you will come at last to love the whole world with an all-embracing love.

Fyodor Dostoyevsky

Every situation — no, every moment — is of infinite worth; for it is the representative of a whole eternity.

⚬

J. W. von Goethe

Learn to value yourself, which means: to fight for your happiness.

—— ❧ ——

Ayn Rand

If this invisible germ of life in the grain of wheat can thus pass unimpaired through three thousand resurrections, I shall not doubt that my soul has power to clothe itself with a new body, suited to its new existence, when this earthly frame has crumbled into dust.

∞

William Jennings Bryan

Holy" has the same root as "wholly"; it means complete. A man is not complete in spiritual stature if all his mind, heart, soul, strength are not given to God.

☙

R. J. H. Stewart

The love we give away is the only love we keep.

— ✿ —

Elbert Hubbard

Sorrows gather around great souls as storms do around mountains; but like them, they break the storm and purify the air of the plain beneath them.

❧

Jean Paul Richter

That happiness which belongs to a mind which by deep meditation has been washed clear of all impurity and has entered within the Self, cannot be described by words; it can be felt by the inward power only.

ॐ

Maitranyana Brahmana Upanishad

Q. What counsel do you give to the young men who are fighting a losing battle with their lower selves and come to you for advice?

A. Simply prayer. One must humble oneself utterly and look beyond oneself for strength.

Q. But what if the young men complain that their prayer is not heard?

A. To want an answer to one's prayer is to tempt God. If prayer fails to bring relief, it is only lip-prayer. If prayer does not help, nothing else will. One must go on ceaselessly. This, then, is my message to the youth. In spite of themselves, the youth must believe in the all-conquering power of Love and Truth.

Mohandas K. Gandhi

A holy person is one who is sanctified by the presence and action of God within him.

⚬⚬

Thomas Merton

Love cures people, the ones who receive love and the ones who give it, too.

— ✦ —

Karl A. Menninger

It is . . . in plunging into the stream of life itself and entering into the deepest involvement with the values that confront us, exercising our wills to the utmost—to the breaking point—that we find God in the very extremity of the battle.

❧

Geddes MacGregor

Each flower is a soul

opening out to nature.

— ❧ —

Gérard de Nerval

Duty becomes a disease with us; it drags us ever forward.... This duty, this idea of duty is the midday summer sun which scorches the innermost soul of mankind.... The only true duty is to be unattached and to work as free beings, to give up all work unto God.

ख़

Swami Vivekananda

Faith, like light, should always be simple
and unbending; while love, like warmth,
should beam forth on every side, and bend
to every necessity of our brethren.

∞

Martin Luther

The course of nature is the art of God.

— ❧ —

Edward Young

Love is to the moral nature exactly what the sun is to the earth.

— ✿ —

Honoré de Balzac

God allows us to experience the low points of life in order to teach us lessons we could not learn in any other way. The way we learn those lessons is not to deny the feelings but to find the meanings underlying them.

Stanley Lindquist

The place where man vitally finds God . . . is within his own experience of goodness, truth, and beauty, and the truest images of God are therefore to be found in man's spiritual life.

Harry Emerson Fosdick

In prayer a man should always unite himself with the community.

— ✣ —

The Talmud

Love is the vital essence that pervades and permeates, from the center to the circumference, the graduating circles of all thought and action. Love is the talisman of human weal and woe—the open sesame to every human soul.

ဢ

Elizabeth Cady Stanton

In prayer we shift the center of living from self-consciousness to self-surrender.

— ❧ —

Abraham Joshua Heschel

We are members of one great body, planted by nature in a mutual love, and fitted for a social life. We must consider that we were born for the good of the whole.

ოა

Seneca

Give humanity hope and it will dare
and suffer joyfully, not counting the cost—
hope with laughter on her banner and on
her face the fresh beauty of morning.

ॐ

John Elof Boodin

Silence is not a thing we make; it is something into which we enter. It is always there. We talk about keeping silence. We keep only that which is precious. Silence is precious, for it is of God. In silence all God's acts are done; in silence alone can his voice be heard and his word spoken.

ಣ

Mother Maribel

By the law of love, above every other law, men ought to live. It provides the constraining dynamic for spiritual and moral achievement. God gave the law and to live by it is to live on the highest level of human experience.

ଧୋଷ

Clifton J. Allen

Man is close to God when he is close to the people. If we think of God as something in favor of the betterment of man, both materially and spiritually, and if we act in a way that brings about that betterment—if we do not cling to riches, selfishness, or greed—then I believe we are getting closer to God.

ໜ

Daniel Ortega

Life is a mission. Every other definition of life is false, and leads all who accept it astray. Religion, science, philosophy, though still at variance upon many points, all agree in this, that every existence is an aim.

 න

Giuseppe Mazzini

We are not sent into this world to do anything into which we cannot put our hearts.

——— ⚬ ———

John Ruskin

To be human is to be challenged to be more divine. Not even to try to meet such a challenge is the biggest defeat imaginable.

Maya Angelou

The authentic insight and experience of any human soul, were it but insight and experience in hewing of wood and drawing of water, is real knowledge, a real possession and acquirement.

က

Thomas Carlyle

We are but shadows: we are not endowed with real life, and all that seems most real about us is but the thinnest substance of a dream,—till the heart be touched. That touch creates us—then we begin to be—thereby we are beings of reality and inheritors of eternity.

დი

Nathaniel Hawthorne

God does not die on the day when we
cease to believe in a personal deity, but
we die on the day when our lives cease
to be illuminated by the steady radiance,
renewed daily, of a wonder, the source
of which is beyond all reason.

∞

Dag Hammarskjöld

A spiritual truth is valid only when it does not contradict universal reason, one's inner experience, and the experience of other seers of truth.

ॐ

Swami Nikhilananda

The universe is but one great city, full of beloved ones, divine and human by nature, endeared to each other.

— ∞ —

Epictetus

Until you know that life is interesting — and find it so — you haven't found your soul.

———— ✠ ————

Geoffrey Fisher

Detachment is not a denial of life
but a denial of death; not a disintegration
but the condition of wholeness; not a refusal
to love but the determination to
love truly, deeply, and fully.

∽

Gerald Vann

Men exist for the sake of one another. Teach them then or bear with them.

— ✦ —

Marcus Aurelius

What I am actually saying is that we *each* need to let our intuition guide us, and then be willing to follow that guidance directly and fearlessly.

∞

Shakti Gawain

Let me not pray to be sheltered from dangers but to be
fearless in facing them.
Let me not beg for the stilling of my pain but for the heart to
conquer it.
Let me not look for allies in life's battlefield but to my own
strength.
Let me not crave in anxious fear to be saved but hope for the
patience to win my freedom.
Grant me that I may not be a coward, feeling your mercy in
my success alone; but let me find the grasp of your
hand in my failure.

Rabindranath Tagore

Be good yourself and the world will be good.

— ❧ —

Hindu proverb

Only when we feel that through all
our vicissitudes some unfathomable purpose
runs, and that by meeting life nobly
and courageously we can co-operate in
the fulfillment of that purpose, do we
find peace.

ΩΩ

Alice Hegan Rice

What nature delivers to us is never stale. Because what nature creates has eternity in it.

— ✠ —

Isaac Bashevis Singer

Never to tire, never to grow cold; to be patient, sympathetic, tender; to look for the budding flower and the opening heart; to hope always, like God, to love always—this is duty.

ॐ

H. F. Amiel

As the bird alights on the bough,
then plunges into the air again, so the
thoughts of God pause but for
a moment in any form.

ॐ

Ralph Waldo Emerson

The spirit is the true self,
not that physical figure
which can be pointed out by
your finger.

— ✠ —

Cicero

When all our efforts have come to nothing, we naturally tend to doubt not just ourselves, but also whether God is just. At those moments, our only hope is to seek every evidence that God *is* just, by communing with the people we know who are strongest in their faith.

Bill Moyers

The finest test of character is seen in the amount and the power of gratitude we have.

— ✣ —

Milo H. Gates

People who pray for miracles usually don't get miracles. ... But people who pray for courage, for strength to bear the unbearable, for the grace to remember what they have left instead of what they have lost, very often find their prayers answered. ... Their prayers helped them tap hidden reserves of faith and courage which were not available to them before.

Harold S. Kushner

When one finds one's
Self, one has found
God; and finding God
one has found one's Self.

———— ∞ ————

Anandamayi Ma

In form, the word "God" is small indeed, but in meaning it is infinite. It expresses the greatest thought that ever entered the heart of man. It is lisped by the children, read and known of all men; but also inscribed at the zenith of the universe, and shedding its glory on all below it.

ॐ

Harry William Everest

158

No one can get inner peace by pouncing on it, by vigorously willing to have it. Peace is a margin of power around our daily need. Peace is a consciousness of springs too deep for earthly droughts to dry up. Peace is the gift not of volitional struggle but of spiritual hospitality.

୨୧

Harry Emerson Fosdick

The first duty of love

is to listen.

———— ❧ ————

Paul Tillich

I believe that man will not merely endure; he will prevail. He is immortal, not because he alone among creatures has an inexhaustible voice, but because he has a soul, a spirit capable of compassion and sacrifice and endurance.

∽

William Faulkner

Neglect not the gift

that is in thee.

— ❧ —

I Timothy 4:14

I like to speak of prayer as listening. We live in a culture that is terribly afraid to listen. We'd prefer to remain deaf. The Latin root word of the word "deaf" is "absurd." Prayer means moving from absurdity to obedience. Let the words descend from your head to your heart so you can begin to know God. In prayer, you become who you are meant to be.

Henri Nouwen

Faith is the heart of

the mind.

———— ∞ ————

Anonymous

The life of sensation is the life of greed; it requires more and more. The life of the spirit requires less and less; time is ample and its passage sweet.

ಲಾ

Annie Dillard

Kindness in words creates confidence. Kindness in thinking creates profoundness. Kindness in giving creates love.

— ❧ —

Lao-tzu

We do not walk to God with the feet of our body, nor would wings, if we had them, carry us to Him, but we go to Him by the affections of our soul.

ა

St. Augustine

The idea of God, and the sense of His presence, intensify all noble feeling and encourage all noble effort, pour new life into our languid love, and give firmness to our vacillating purpose.

∞

George Eliot

There is a God within us,

and we glow when

He stirs us.

— ✦ —

Ovid

It isn't so urgent ... whether you believe in God as whether he can believe in you. If you will conduct yourself in a manner that might encourage him to believe in you, the time may come when you feel that you should return the compliment.

ഇരു

Lloyd Douglas

You know that if you get in the water and have nothing to hold on to, but try to behave as you would on dry land, you will drown. But if, on the other hand, you trust yourself to the water and let go, you will float. And this is exactly the situation of faith.

∽

Alan Watts

Perhaps nature is our best

assurance of

immortality.

———— ❧ ————

Eleanor Roosevelt

Naturally, we cannot say much about the spiritual body, because we cannot imagine what it would be like to have a spiritual body different from that which we now inhabit; but it seems to me reasonable to believe that we are weaving our spiritual bodies as we go along.

ಐ

W. R. Matthews

Teach him [your child] to live rather than to avoid death; life is not breath, but action, the use of our senses, our mind, our faculties, every part of ourselves which makes us conscious of our living. Life consists less in length of days than in the keen sense of living.

ॐ

Jean-Jacques Rousseau

The greatest prayer is patience.

※

Gautama Buddha

God is to me that creative Force, behind and in the universe, who manifests Himself as energy, as life, as order, as beauty, as thought, as conscience, as love.

ഇരു

Henry Sloane Coffin

Faith is the sense of life, that sense by virtue of which man does not destroy himself, but continues to live on. It is the force whereby we live.

ဢ

Leo Tolstoy

Waves of serener life pass over us from time to time, like flakes of sunlight over the fields in cloudy weather.

— ❧ —

Henry David Thoreau

Not truth, but faith it is

that keeps the world alive.

— ✸ —

Edna St. Vincent Millay

To infinite, ever-present Love,
all is Love, and there is no error,
no sin, sickness, nor death.

❧

Mary Baker Eddy

What I know of the divine science and Holy Scripture I learnt in woods and fields.

— ❧ —

St. Bernard of Clairvaux

An old mystic says somewhere, "God is an unutterable sigh in the innermost depths of the soul." With still greater justice, we may reverse the proposition, and say the soul is a never ending sigh after God.

❧

Theodor Christlieb

I believe in God and in His wisdom and benevolence.

—— ❧ ——

John Adams

Faith means being grasped by a power
that is greater than we are, a power that
shakes us and turns us, and transforms and
heals us. Surrender to this power of faith.

∞

Paul Tillich

The man who has seen the rising moon
break out of the clouds at midnight has
been present like an archangel at the
creation of light and of the world.

❧

Ralph Waldo Emerson

Our prayers should be for blessings in general, for God knows best what is good for us.

— ❧ —

Socrates

There is not a heart but has its moments of longing, yearning for something better, nobler, holier than it knows now.

— ❧ —

Henry Ward Beecher

It is meditation that leads us in spirit into the hallowed solitudes wherein we find God alone—in peace, in calm, in silence, in recollection .

ॐ

J. Crasset

Spirituality for me is the sum total of all the acts of my day, waking with a prayer, eating kosher, sharing with my friends, even, in my mother's constellation, taking out the garbage. Judaism makes everything holy, ties me back to history and connects me with the spirit of God.

❧

Ari Goldman

The beginning of faith is practically empty of content. It is pure trust.

— ❧ —

Brother David Steindl-Rast

[*Love is*] the joy of
the good, the wonder of the
wise, the amazement
of the gods.

— ❦ —

Plato

Nor let soft slumber close your eyes
Before you've recollected thrice
The train of actions through the day:
Where have my feet chose out the way?
What have I learnt where'er I've been
From all I've heard, from all I've seen?
What know I more that's worth the knowing?
What have I done that's worth the doing?
What have I sought that I should shun?
What duty have I left undone;
Or into what new follies run?
These self inquiries are the road
That leads us to virtue and to God.

Isaac Watts

God hears no sweeter music than the cracked chimes of the courageous human spirit ringing in imperfect acknowledgment of His perfect love.

ಐ

Joshua Loth Liebman

Faith faces everything that makes the world uncomfortable—pain, fear, loneliness, shame, death—and acts with a compassion by which these things are transformed, even exalted.

இஒ

Samuel H. Miller

Happiness is an expression of the soul in considered actions.

— ✿ —

Aristotle

Certain thoughts are prayers. There are moments when, whatever be the attitude of the body, the soul is on its knees.

—— ∞ ——

Victor Hugo

Not holiness alone, but the beauty of holiness, is required to bind our hearts, our whole souls to God.

———— ✣ ————

Bede Jarrett

Solitude is not something you must hope for in the future. Rather, it is a deepening of the present, and unless you look for it in the present you will never find it.

Thomas Merton

A sublime hope cheers ever the faithful
heart, that elsewhere, in other regions of the
universal powers, souls are now acting,
enduring and daring, which can love us,
and which we can love.

∞

Ralph Waldo Emerson

We think we must climb to a certain height of goodness before we can reach God. But . . . if we are in a hole the Way begins in the hole. The moment we set our face in the same direction as His, we are walking with God.

༄

Helen Wodehouse

The soul should always stand ajar, ready to welcome the ecstatic experience.

— ❧ —

Emily Dickinson

The fact of our being able to form
abstract or universal ideas is, in itself,
a proof of the immateriality, or, as it is
technically called, the spirituality of the
soul, a proof that the soul is, in its essence,
independent of matter.

∞

Richard Downey

When we, as individuals,

first rediscover our spirit,

we are usually drawn

to nurture and cultivate

this awareness.

———— ∞ ————

Shakti Gawain

God is what man finds that is divine in himself. God is the best way man can behave in the ordinary occasions of life, and the farthest point to which man can stretch himself.

৩৩

Max Lerner

Faith is raising the sail of our little boat
until it is caught up in the soft winds above
and picks up speed, not from anything
within itself, but from the vast resources
of the universe around us.

❧

Ralph W. Ward, Jr.

Because you cannot see him, God is everywhere.

❦

Yasunari Kawabata

Any God I ever felt in church I brought in with me.

— 🐚 —

Alice Walker

In its highest sense [the soul is] a vast capacity for God. . . . A chamber with elastic and contractile walls, which can be expanded, with God as its guest, illimitably, but which without God shrinks and shrinks until every vestige of the Divine is gone, and God's image is kept without God's Spirit.

☙

Henry Drummond

To understand everything is to forgive everything.

❧

Gautama Buddha

May you live all the days of your life.

— ❧❧ —

Jonathan Swift

How good is man's life, the mere
living! how fit to employ
All the heart and the soul and the sense
forever in joy!

ভ০৪

Robert Browning

The man who has no inner life is the slave of his surroundings.

— ❧ —

Henri Frédéric Amiel

You are as prone to love as the sun is to shine; it being the most delightful and natural employment of the Soul of Man: without which you are dark and miserable. For certainly he that delights not in Love makes vain the universe, and is of necessity to himself the greatest burden.

∞

Thomas Traherne

One wears his mind out in study,
and yet has more mind with which to study.
One gives away his heart in love,
and yet has more heart to give away. One
perishes out of pity for a suffering world,
and is the stronger therefore. So, too, it is
possible at one and the same time to
hold life and let it go.

∞

Milton Steinberg

Love is an image of God, and not a lifeless image, but the living essence of the divine nature which beams full of all goodness.

✸✸

Martin Luther

Holiness is a greater ideal by far
than happiness because it embraces struggle
and sees all things—achievement, aspiration,
even love—as part of the moral drama
of the world and not as life's end or sole
reason for being.

∽

David Wolpe

What else is nature but God?

— ✿ —

Seneca

The Unknown Cause of the universe is Himself a Spirit, whose Word is perfect truth, whose nature is perfect righteousness, whose law is perfect love.

∞

Washington Gladden

To me every hour of
the light and dark
is a miracle,
Every cubic inch of space
is a miracle.

—— ∾ ——

Walt Whitman

Prayer is the world

in tune.

— ❦ —

Henry Vaughan

God is infallible in His own nature: He cannot be subject to error or sin, for He is His own light, and His own law; reason is consubstantial with Him, He understands it perfectly, and loves it invincibly.

சு

Nicholas Malebranche

Trust in God and do something.

❧

Mary Lyon

If you have a particular faith or religion, that is good. But you can survive without it if you have love, compassion, and tolerance. The clear proof of a person's love of God is if that person genuinely shows love to fellow human beings.

ೞ

Dalai Lama

The secret of contentment is the realization that life is a gift, right.

— ✺ —

Anonymous

Love rules the court, the camp,
the grove,
And men below, and saints above;
For love is heaven, and heaven is love.

ॐ

Sir Walter Scott

Let the Divine Mind flow through your own mind, and you will be happier. I have found the greatest power in the world in the power of prayer. There is no shadow of doubt of that. I speak from my own experience.

☙❧

Cecil B. DeMille

Let love be genuine; hate what is evil, hold fast to what is good; love one another with brotherly affection; outdo one another in showing honor. Never flag in zeal, be aglow with the Spirit, serve the Lord. Rejoice in your hope, be patient in tribulation, be constant in prayer.

✄

Romans 12:9-12

Sometimes I think that just not thinking of oneself is a form of prayer....

— ✿ —

Barbara Grizzuti Harrison

All are but parts of one
stupendous whole,
Whose body Nature is, and
God the soul.

— ❧ —

Alexander Pope

The person who has not learned to be happy and content while completely alone for an hour a day, or a week has missed life's greatest serenity.

∽

H. Clay Tate

Now that my heart is closed against all desire for earthly things, now that I have no longer any sense for the transitory and perishable, the universe appears before my eyes clothed in a more glorious form.

ოი

J. G. Fichte

Do not let trifles disturb your tranquillity of mind.... Life is too precious to be sacrificed for the nonessential and transient.... Ignore the inconsequential.

ა

Grenville Kleiser

Joy is the echo of Gods life within us.

Joseph Marmion

Prayer . . . is . . . a technique for contacting and learning to know Reality . . . the exploration of Reality by exploring the Beyond, which is within.

Gerald Heard

The greatest happiness of life is the conviction that we are loved—loved for ourselves, or rather, loved in spite of ourselves.

ॐ

Victor Hugo

All I have seen

teaches me to trust the

creator for all I

have not seen.

❧

Ralph Waldo Emerson

You can keep a faith only as you can keep a plant, by rooting it into your life and making it grow there.

૪૭

Phillips Brooks

Those things that nature denied to human sight, she revealed to the eyes of the soul.

— ❧ —

Ovid

If everything is coming your way, you are probably in the wrong lane. Adversity and defeat are more conducive to spiritual growth than prosperity and victory.

ဆော

John Steinbeck

The divine essence itself is love and wisdom.

— ❧ —

Emanuel Swedenborg

Instead of allowing yourself to be so unhappy, just let your love grow as God wants it to grow; seek goodness in others, love more persons more; love them more impersonally, more unselfishly, without thought of return. The return, never fear, will take care of itself.

ගඟ

Henry Drummond

Love, like the opening of the heavens to the saints, shows for a moment, even to the dullest man, the possibilities of the human race. He has faith, hope, and charity for another being, perhaps but the creation of his imagination; still it is a great advance for a man to be profoundly loving, even in his imagination.

Sir Arthur Helps

Be not forgetful of prayer. Every time you pray, if your prayer is sincere, there will be new feeling and new meaning in it, which will give you fresh courage, and you will understand that prayer is an education.

ဆော

Fyodor Dostoyevsky

Love is the doorway through which the human soul passes from selfishness to service and from solitude to kinship with all mankind.

❧

Anonymous

Prayer is and remains always a native and deepest impulse of the soul of man.

— ✿ —

Thomas Carlyle

Life is a pure flame,
and we live by an
invisible sun within us.

———— ❧ ————

Thomas Browne

Divine love is a sacred flower, which in its early bud is happiness, and in its full bloom is heaven.

❧

Eleanor Louisa Hervey

Though our natural life were no life, but rather a continual dying, yet we have two lives besides that, an eternal life reserved for heaven, but yet a heavenly life too, a spiritual life, even in this world.

സ

John Donne

What is hope? Hope is *wishing* for a thing to come true; faith is *believing* that it will come true. Hope is wanting something so eagerly that—in spite of all the evidence that you're not going to get it—you go right on wanting it. And the remarkable thing about it is that this very act of hoping produces a kind of strength of its own.

Norman Vincent Peale

Faith consists in being vitally concerned with that ultimate reality to which I give the symbolical name of God. Whoever reflects earnestly on the meaning of life is on the verge of an act of faith.

ဢၢ

Paul Tillich

Be good, keep your feet dry, your eyes open, your heart at peace, and your soul in the joy of Christ.

— ❧ —

Thomas Merton

The purpose of life is the quest for truth.

❧

Daniel L. Thrapp

The ultimate standpoint of Zen, therefore, is that we have been led astray through ignorance to find a split in our own being, that there was from the very beginning no need for a struggle between the finite and the infinite, that the peace we are seeking so eagerly after has been there all the time.

D. T. Suzuki

The body, that is but dust; the soul, it is a bud of eternity.

Nathaniel Culverwel

We need God, not in order to understand the *why*, but in order to feel and sustain the ultimate *wherefore*, to give a meaning to the Universe.

∞

Miguel de Unamuno

Keep your faith in all beautiful things; in the sun when it is hidden, in the Spring when it is gone.

— ✦ —

Roy R. Gilson

He who sincerely praises God will soon discover within his soul an inclination to praise goodness in his fellow man.

Oliver G. Wilson

Every happening, great and small, is a parable whereby God speaks to us, and the art of life is to get the message.

❧

Malcolm Muggeridge

If you can't have faith in what is held up to you for faith, you must find things to believe in yourself, for a life without faith in something is too narrow a space to live.

ဆာ

George E. Woodbury

He who prays must commit himself and his wants to the transforming power of God. He must seek what is genuinely the greatest good and not merely the specific things which will satisfy his present wants.

Henry N. Wieman

Let a man begin with an earnest "I ought," and if he perseveres, by God's grace he will end in the free blessedness of "I will." Let him force himself to abound in small acts of duty, and he will, by and by, find them the joyous habit of his soul.

F. W. Robertson

God is a being absolutely infinite; a substance consisting of infinite attributes, each of which expresses His eternal and infinite essence.

Baruch Spinoza

There are four things in which every man must interest himself. Who am I? Wherefore have I come from? Whither am I going? How long shall I be here? All spiritual inquiry begins with these questions and attempts to find out the answers.

കൈ

Diana Baskin

God lies ahead. . . .

He depends on us. It is

through us that God

is achieved.

———— ❧ ————

André Gide

Your actions in passing,
pass not away, for every good
work is a grain of seed for
eternal life.

— ✠ —

St. Bernard of Clairvaux

There is only one corner of the universe you can be certain of improving, and that's your own self.

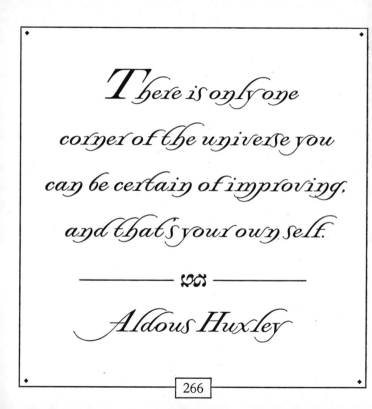

Aldous Huxley

Spirit unites itself inwardly to soul and transfigures it. The distinction between spirit and soul does not imply their separation.

∽

Nicholas Berdyaev

Find the seed at the bottom of your heart and bring forth a flower.

❧

Shigenori Kameoka

It is a great mistake to suppose that God is only, or even chiefly, concerned with religion.

❦

William Temple

I am certainly convinced that it is one of
the greatest impulses of mankind to arrive
at something higher than a natural state.

ഇം

James Baldwin

Nature is the art of God.

— ❦ —

Dante

I want ... to borrow from the language of the saints ... to live "in grace" as much of the time as possible. By "grace" I mean an inner harmony, essentially spiritual, which can be translated into outward harmony. I would like to achieve a state of inner spiritual grace from which I could function and give as I was meant to in the eye of God.

Anne Morrow Lindbergh

No one has the capacity to judge God. We are drops in that limitless ocean of mercy.

❧

Mohandas K. Gandhi

To pray is to descend with the mind
into the heart, and there to stand before
the face of the Lord, ever-present, all-seeing,
within you.

Theophan the Recluse

Goodness is love in action, love with its hand to the plow, love with the burden on its back, love following his footsteps who went about continually doing good.

ಬಾ

James Hamilton

Given the hardest terms, supposing our days are indeed but a shadow, even so, we may well adorn and beautify, in scrupulous self-respect, our souls, and whatever our souls touch upon.

∞

Walter Pater

To the poet, to the philosopher,
to the saint, all things are friendly and
sacred, all events profitable, all days holy,
all men divine.

∞

Ralph Waldo Emerson

Live truth instead of professing it.

— ✣ —

Elbert Hubbard

Throughout this varied and eternal world Soul is the only element.

Percy Bysshe Shelley

Our motive for prayer must be the divine will, not our own.

❦

D. Lawrence Scupoli

Prayer is not a substitute for work;
it is a desperate effort to work further
and to be efficient beyond the range
of one's powers.

ॐ

George Santayana

The passionate yearning which is poured forth in prayer does not spring from man's narrow heart, but from God's eternal love to allure and draw man upward toward Himself.

❧

Friedrich Heiler

Reduce the complexity of life by eliminating the needless wants of life, and the labors of life reduce themselves.

—— ✺ ——

Edwin Way Teale

Prayer is nought but a rising desire of the heart into God by withdrawing of the heart from all earthly thoughts.

— ✣ —

Walter Hylton

Prayer is a definite act of the mind—
a gesture by which the human spirit seeks
out the spirit of the universe. In prayer you
call upon the Infinite to help. Prayer is far
less a thing "asked for" than it is a thing
"done"—a reaching forth to link oneself
to the sources of celestial power.

෮ඟ

William C. Taggart

The soul is the mirror of an indestructible universe.

❧

G. W. Leibniz

Mental prayer is nothing else . . . but being on terms of friendship with God, frequently conversing in secret with Him.

— ❧ —

St. Teresa of Avila

For silence is not God, not speaking is not God, fasting is not God, nor eating is not God; loneliness is not God, nor company is not God; nor yet any of all the other two such contraries. He is hid between them, and may not be found by any work of thy soul, but all only by love of thine heart.

The Cloud of Unknowing

It is only the souls that do not love that go empty in this world.

— ∞ —

Robert Hugh Benson

Happiness lies in the absorption in some vocation which satisfies the soul.

— ✿ —

Sir William Osler

We have never made a better prayer than when, after having made it, we do not know how it was made, since that is a sure sign that our soul was so attached to God as not to have had enough attention left to reflect upon itself.

ოთ

Père Hayneuve

And we shall be made truly wise if we be made content; content, too, not only with what we can understand, but content with what we do not understand—the habit of mind which theologians call—and rightly—faith in God.

❧

Charles Kingsley

Wonder is the basis

of worship.

— ✠ —

Thomas Carlyle

To comprehend the truth rationality itself must conform to all the laws of the spiritual world . . . and be related to all the vital and moral forces of the spirit.

✖

Aleksei Khonyskov

Cultivate solitude and quiet and a
few sincere friends, rather than mob
merriment, noise, and thousands of
nodding acquaintances.

William Powell

Prayer should be understood, not as a mere mechanical recitation of formulas, but as a mystical elevation, an absorption of consciousness in the contemplation of a principle both permeating and transcending our world.

ॐ

Alexis Carrel

Religious faith is not a storm cellar to which men and women can flee for refuge from the storms of life. It is, instead, an inner spiritual strength which enables them to face those storms with hope and serenity. Religious faith has the miraculous power to lift ordinary human beings to greatness in seasons of stress.

Sam J. Ervin, Jr.

We can never see Christianity from the catechism: —from the pastures, from a boat in the pond, from amidst the songs of woodbirds, we possibly may.

Ralph Waldo Emerson

Once you accept the existence of God—however you define him, however you explain your relationship to him—then you are caught forever with his presence in the center of all things.

Morris West

If you tell the truth, you have
infinite power supporting you; but if not,
you have infinite power against you.

*General Charles
"Chinese" Gordon*

Faith is not merely praying
Upon our knees at night;
Faith is not merely straying
Through darkness into light;
Faith is not merely waiting
For glory that may be.
Faith is the brave endeavor,
The splendid enterprise,
The strength to serve, whatever
Conditions may arise.

Anonymous

Prayer is not a monologue. It speaks to God and to the community. In the last analysis, religion is not what goes on inside a soul. It is what goes on in the world, between people, between us and God. To trap faith in a monologue, and pretend that it resides solely inside the self, undermines the true interchange of all belief.

David J. Wolpe

God is day and night,
winter and summer, war
and peace, satiety and want.

— ✿ —

Heraclitus

Happiness is neither within us only, or without us; it is the union of ourselves with God.

— ✿ —

Blaise Pascal

Bodily pain affects man as a whole down to the deepest layers of his moral being. It forces him to face again the fundamental questions of his fate, of his attitude toward God and fellow man, of his individual and collective responsibility and of the sense of his pilgrimage on earth.

Pope Pius XII

God is a spirit; and they that worship him must worship him in spirit and in truth.

—— ❧ ——

John 4:24

Love is will, the will to share your happiness with all. Being happy—making happy—this is the rhythm of love.

ॐ

Nasaragada Ha Maharaj

Pray only for the suppression of evil, and never for one's material well-being, for a separating veil arises if one admits the material into the spiritual.

ॐ

Rabbi Israel Baal Shem-Tov

There is a land of the living and a land of the dead and the bridge is love, the only survival, the only meaning.

⬥

Thornton Wilder

Man does not *have* a soul; he *is* one.

భా

Harold Bruce Hunting

Our prayer for others ought never to be: "God, give them the light Thou hast given to me!" but: "God! Give to them all the light and truth they need for their highest development!"

∞

Mohandas K. Gandhi

Man discovers his own wealth when God comes to ask gifts of him.

—— ✷ ——

Rabindranath Tagore

Hope is the thing with feathers
That perches in the soul,
And sings the tune without the words,
And never stops at all.

∞

Emily Dickinson

As a coal is revived by incense, prayer revives the hope of the heart.

&

J. W. von Goethe

The soul has in itself a capacity for affection, and loves just as naturally as it perceives, understands, and remembers.

Plutarch

You pray in your distress and in
your need; would that you might pray
also in the fullness of your joy and in
your days of abundance.

ಬಚ

Kahlil Gibran

Give spiritual strength to people and they will give genuine affection to you.

— ❧ —

Anonymous

Prayer is our humble answer to the inconceivable surprise of living.

— ❧ —

Abraham Joshua Heschel

Love is a symbol of eternity. It wipes out all sense of time, destroying all memory of a beginning and all fear of an end.

ೞ

Madame de Staël

The universe is a single life comprising one substance and one soul.

❧

Marcus Aurelius

The spiritual life is not a thing without emotions. The saints weep at the thought of their own sins and the goodness of God; their hearts beat to the bursting point within them, they shout and dance for joy; they die to see God.

ॐ

Jean Mouroux

We are born to inquire after truth; it belongs to a greater power to possess it. It is not, as Democritus said, hid in the bottom of the deeps, but rather elevated to an infinite height in the divine knowledge.

಄಄

Michel de Montaigne

Love is the doorway through which the human soul passes from selfishness to service and from solitude to kinship with all mankind.

℘

Anonymous

When we pray for another, it is not an attempt to alter God's mind toward him. In prayer we add our wills to God's good will . . . that in fellowship with Him He and we may minister to those whom both He and we love.

ༀ

Henry Sloane Coffin

Love is that orbit of the restless soul
Whose circle graces the confines of space,
Bounding within the limits of its race
Utmost extremes.

☙

George Henry Boker

Faith is an awareness of divine mutuality and companionship, a form of communion between God and man.

— ❦ —

Abraham Joshua Heschel

Your success and happiness lie in you. External conditions are the accidents of life. The great enduring realities are love and service. Joy is the holy fire that keeps our purpose warm and our intelligence aglow. Resolve to keep happy, and your joy and you shall form an invincible host against difficulty.

Helen Keller

Think truly, and thy thoughts
Shall the world's famine feed.
Speak truly, and each word of thine
Shall be a fruitful seed.
Live truly, and thy life shall be
A great and noble creed.

Horatius Bonar

I believe that God prays in us and through us, whether we are praying or not (and whether we believe in God or not). So, any prayer on my part is a conscious response to what God is already doing in my life.

ෆ

Malcolm Boyd

Love isn't like a reservoir. You'll never drain it dry. It's much more like a natural spring. The longer and the farther it flows, the stronger and the deeper and the clearer it becomes.

ℭ

Eddie Cantor

When we pray, we link ourselves with the inexhaustible power that spins the universe. We ask that a part of this power be apportioned to our needs. Even in asking, our human deficiencies are filled and we arise strengthened and repaired.

ಐ

Alexis Carrel

We are all born for love; it is the principle of existence and its only end.

— ✢ —

Benjamin Disraeli

In the time of your life, live—so that in that good time there shall be no ugliness or death for yourself or for any life your life touches. Seek goodness everywhere, and where it is found, bring it out of its hiding place and let it be free and unashamed.

William Saroyan

The Infinite Goodness has such wide arms that it takes whatever turns to it.

— ∞ —

Dante

The virtue of poverty means complete detachment; we are not to depend on things, but they on us. . . . You will get detachment from things and from self by merely giving yourself to God, and accepting yourself as you find yourself to be.

ജ

John Chapman

Greatness is a spiritual condition worthy to excite love, interest, and admiration, and the outward proof of possessing greatness is that we excite love, interest, and admiration.

ಞ

Matthew Arnold

Our whole being subsists in virtue of the subsistence of the spiritual soul which is in us a principle of creative unity, independence, and liberty.

Jacques Maritain

When you pray for anyone you tend to modify your personal attitude toward him. You lift the relationship thereby to a higher level. The best in the other person begins to flow out toward you as your best flows toward him. In the meeting of the best in each a higher unity of understanding is established.

Norman Vincent Peale

Touch the earth, love the earth,
honour the earth, her plains, her valleys,
her hills, and her seas; rest your spirit in her
solitary places.

தை

Henry Beston

To be spiritually minded

is life and peace.

— ❧ —

Romans 8:6

The man who, casting off all desires, lives free from attachment; who is free from egoism and from the feeling that this or that is mine, obtains tranquillity.

જી

Bhagavad-Gita

Faith has to do with the basis,
the ground on which we stand. Hope is
reaching out for something to come.
Love is just being there and acting.

∞

Emil Brunner

The act of praying centers attention on the higher emotion, unifies the spirit, crystallizes emotions, clarifies the judgments, releases latent powers, reinforces confidence that what needs to be done can be done.

∞

Georgia Harkness

It is God in the house when the curtains lift gently at the windows, and a young child sucks his itching gums. We do not understand the mysteries of God. God the winter. Summer, Septembers. Moody dark tones of fathers dying. The splash and laughter. Children playing.

Ellease Southerland

In spite of all our hopes, dreams, and efforts, change is real and forever. Accept it fearlessly. Investigate the unknown; neither fear nor worship it.

ಬಡ

Joseph A. Bauer

Prayer is the spirit

speaking truth

to truth.

───── ✲ ─────

Philip James Bailey

Believe all the good you can of everyone. Do not measure others by yourself. If they have advantages which you have not, let your liberality keep pace with their good fortune.

ളൗ

William Hazlitt

No one may forsake his neighbor when he is in trouble. Everybody is under obligation to help and support his neighbor as he would himself like to be helped.

Martin Luther

Prayer is essentially about making the heart strong so that fear cannot penetrate there.

— ❧ —

Matthew Fox

Prayer is the greatest of spells, the best healing of all spells. . . . Amongst all remedies this one is the healing one that heals with the Holy Word.

✿

Zend-Avesta

This Being of mine, whatever it really is, consists of a little flesh, a little breath, and the ruling reason.

※

Marcus Aurelius

By having reverence for life, we enter into a spiritual relation with the world.

Albert Schweitzer

Happiness lies in the fulfillment of the spirit through the body.

— ❧ —

Cyril Connolly

The prayer that reforms the sinner and heals the sick is an absolute faith that all things are possible to God—a spiritual understanding of Him, an unselfed love.

ⓈⓈ

Mary Baker Eddy

When God loves a creature he wants the creature to know the highest happiness and the deepest misery . . . He wants him to know all that being alive can bring. That is his best gift. . . . There is no happiness save in understanding the whole.

ℳ

Thornton Wilder

In the mystic sense of the creation around us, in the expression of art, in a yearning towards God, the soul grows upward and finds fulfilment of something implanted in its nature.

 හ

Arthur Eddington

Through prayer we can carry in our heart all human pain and sorrow, all conflicts and agonies, all torture and war, all hunger, loneliness, and misery, not because of some great psychological or emotional capacity, but because God's heart has become one with ours.

Henri Nouwen

He who has learned to pray has learned the greatest secret of a holy and happy life.

— ❧ —

William Law

It is the creative potential itself in human beings that is the image of God.

Mary Daly

The longer I live the more beautiful life becomes.

❦

Frank Lloyd Wright

The very movement itself of the soul,
putting itself into a personal relation of
contact with the mysterious power—
of which it feels the presence.

❧

William James

Belief of God is acceptance of the basic principle that the universe makes sense, that there is behind it an ultimate purpose.

ॐ

Carl Wallace Miller

Bad will be the day for every man when he becomes absolutely contented with the life that he is living ... when there is not forever beating at the doors of his soul some great desire to do something larger.

♋

Phillips Brooks

Know then, whatever cheerful and serene
Supports the mind, supports the body too:
Hence, the most vital movement mortals feel
Is hope, the balm and lifeblood of the soul.

ॐ

John Armstrong

Faith is like the little night-light that burns in a sickroom; as long as it is there, the obscurity is not complete, we turn toward it and await the daylight.

ဢ

Abbe Huvelin

The world, the race, the soul—in space
and time the universes,
All bound as is befitting each—all surely
going somewhere.

We are co-creators with God,
not puppets on a string waiting for
something to happen.

ഉര

Leo Booth

And when Love speaks,
the voice of all the gods
Makes heaven drowsy with the harmony.

ॐ

William Shakespeare

The aim of all spiritual practice is love.

ॐ

Sai Baba

For one human being to love another: that is perhaps the most difficult of all our tasks, the ultimate, the last test and proof, the work for which all other work is but preparation.

Rainer Maria Rilke

The main reason for healing is love.

ထက

Paracelsus

The fountain stream of love rises in the love
for an individual, but spreads and falls
in universal love.

Hazrat Inayat Khan